Teen

FAQ

Puberty

Teen FAQ Puberty

Jillian Powell

This edition first published in 2010 by Arcturus Publishing

Distributed by Black Rabbit Books
P.O. Box 3263
Mankato, Minnesota 56002

Copyright © 2010 Arcturus Publishing Limited

Printed in China

Planned and produced by Discovery Books Ltd.
www.discoverybooks.net
Managing editor for Discovery Books: Rachel Tisdale
Editors: Amy Bauman and Juliet Mozley
Designer: D. R. ink
Consultant: Xanthe Fry, School Counselor and Educational Consultant
Picture researcher: Tamsin Osler

Library of Congress Cataloging-in-Publication Data

Powell, Jillian.
   Puberty / Jillian Powell.
      p. cm. -- (Teen FAQ)
   Includes index.
   ISBN 978-1-84837-706-6 (library binding)
   1. Puberty--Juvenile literature. I. Title.
   QP84.4.P69 2011
   612.6'61--dc22

                              2010012715

Picture Credits
Bubbles Photo Library: 6, 37 (Chris Rout). Corbis: cover (Mark Seelen), 11 (James Jeynse), 15 (amanaimages), 16 (Josef Lindau), 17 (Image Source), 21 (Pinto), 42 (Erik Isakson), 43 (Kate Mitchell). Discovery Photo Library: 9 (Chris Fairclough). Getty Images: 19 (Tetra Images), 25 (Datacraft), 26 (David Grossman/Workbook Stock), 30 (John Giustina/Iconica). Istockphoto.com: 23 & 45 (Joselito Briones), 34 (Galina Barskaya), 38 (VMJones), 41 (Linda Kloosterhof). Science Photo Library: 22 (Dr. P. Marazzi). Shutterstock: 7 (Monkey Business Images), 9 right (Lev Olkha), 13 (Magdalena Zurawska), 14 (Monkey Business Images), 29 (Yuri Arcurs), 35 (kojoku), 40 (Martin Novak).

SL001460US
Supplier 03, Date 0510

Contents

1: What's puberty about?   6

2: Body changes: girls   8

3: Body changes: boys   14

4: Skin and hair   20

5: Emotions   26

6: Your body   32

7: Your health   36

Glossary   44

Further information   45

Index   46

1 What's puberty about?

You do your fastest growing during the first year of your life, and then during puberty. About two years before you notice any physical changes, your brain is getting you ready for puberty. Beginning as early as age eight in girls—and two years later, on average, in boys—the brain sends signals for hormonal changes that stimulate puberty. This is the period of physical and sexual development as your body matures into that of an adult.

? WHAT ARE HORMONES?

Hormones are chemicals made by one part of your body (glands) that are carried around in the bloodstream to act on different parts of the body. Hormones work by triggering changes in "target cells," which have special hormone receptors. For example, the pituitary gland makes growth hormones that stimulate the bones in your feet, arms and legs to grow longer.

The chemical changes that trigger puberty begin happening while you are asleep.

The first sign of puberty occurs on average at age 11 in girls, with **menstruation** following about two years later. Signs in boys generally start about two years later, although in some cases puberty may not begin until about the age of 15.

Night action

No one knows why, but puberty begins when you are asleep! Cells in the brain begin sending chemical signals in the form of hormones in your bloodstream. They begin the changes we call puberty.

Growth spurt

Puberty triggers a "growth spurt," and you're suddenly growing bigger and taller. On average, a young person's height increases by around 10 inches (25 cm) during puberty. Many find their arms and legs grow first, making them look and feel a bit "gangly" or clumsy until the rest of the body catches up. You may find you quickly outgrow clothes and shoes and you can feel tired and need more sleep as your body uses energy for growing. Girls keep on growing until they are around 17 years old, and some boys continue growing until they are 19 or 20.

Sex hormones

During puberty, your body is preparing for sex and **reproduction**. Your body begins producing sex hormones. Both boys and girls have a mix of male and female sex hormones, although boys have mainly male hormones and girls have mainly female hormones. These hormones bring about changes not just in the way your body looks but also in how you feel.

"We often have the illusion that we are in control of our bodies. The reality is it is usually our biology that controls us. That is particularly obvious during the great rollercoaster ride of puberty."

Professor Robert Winston, British medical doctor, scientist, television personality, and politician

ORIGIN

One sign of puberty is the increase of body hair in girls and boys. The word "puberty" means to be covered in fine hair and comes from the Latin word *pubescere*, meaning to grow hairy.

Peer groups bond closely as young people share the pleasures and pitfalls of growing up.

FAQ

2 Body changes: girls

If you are a girl, as your body goes into puberty, hormones start to work on your **ovaries** and **adrenal glands** so they begin to produce female sex hormones called **estrogen** and **progesterone**. These hormones bring about changes in your body.

HEALTH WARNING

It is normal and healthy to put on some weight during puberty (see Body weight, page 32). Dieting to lose weight is not advisable unless a doctor has diagnosed a young person as overweight or **obese**. There are many health risks associated with not eating a balanced diet. Lack of vitamins and minerals (many found in fruit and vegetables) can cause problems such as:

- **depression** and irritability
- **anemia**
- tiredness and difficulty sleeping
- aching joints and muscle weakness
- bone and tooth decay
- skin problems
- nausea and vomiting
- headaches.

First signs

The first signs of puberty can begin any time between the ages of 8 to 13. You have a major growth spurt. Your body grows taller and starts to change shape as you become curvier and put on weight around the hips and middle. Your breasts begin to grow, showing as small swellings or "buds" under the nipples.

The **vulva** (the part of the body outside the **vagina**) begins to develop as **labia** (the lips around the vagina) grow. You will also begin to notice a sticky clear or white discharge from your vagina. This can be a sign that your periods (see page 12) will soon start.

More changes

Hair begins to grow under girls' arms and around the pubic area. This normally begins as fine growth and then gets thicker and darker. It may be the same color as hair on the head, but it can also be much lighter or darker. Fine hair growing on the legs can also get darker and coarser during puberty, and some girls may want to start shaving or waxing body hair. Girls will also begin to sweat more, and many choose to start using an underarm deodorant or antiperspirant to avoid body odor (B.O.).

SHAVING OR WAXING?

It is common for girls to want to remove hair from their legs and underarms. Shaving is quickest and cheapest, but it can coarsen the hairs, making them feel prickly. Waxing is another option. It can be painful, but the hair takes longer to grow back. There are also gels and creams, which work by dissolving the hairs to leave the skin feeling smooth.

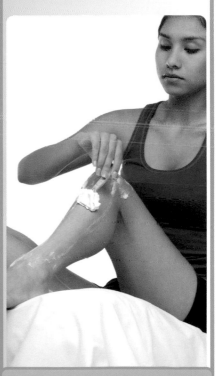

Shaving is a quick and easy method of hair removal for the legs and underarms.

Exercise can help you keep a healthy weight during growth spurts.

What's normal?

As girls go through all the body changes of puberty, they may worry about whether they are "normal," either in the way their bodies look or in how quickly or slowly they are developing.

Breast size

Breasts can begin growing any time between the ages of 8 and 13. Often one grows a bit faster than the other, and although they generally even out, many women continue to have one breast slightly larger than the other. Some girls may worry about being flat-chested or "late developers," but breasts can take up to five years to reach their full size. The nipple and areola (the area around the nipple) also vary in size and in color from light pink through purplish to gray. Nipples can also be brown.

Girls often find it easiest to talk about their worries with friends.

Body parts

During puberty, the vulva develops as the labia grow larger. Girls may worry when they see the inner lips (labia minora) growing longer and fleshier. They may even worry that the growth is abnormal and they are changing sex. But every girl is different. The inner lips can be small and almost hidden or full and fleshy, growing well down below the outer lips. They can be smooth or crinkled, pink, purplish, or brown.

When girls first notice a discharge in their underwear, they may worry that this means they are not "clean," but in fact it is the vagina's way of keeping itself clean and lubricated. To help stay clean, rinse the area with warm water (without soap) and avoid synthetic materials. For example, use cotton underwear instead.

"The timing [of breast development] is determined by your own biological clock that tells your body to start producing high levels of female hormones . . . The final size of a girl's breasts is determined by **heredity** . . . Breast size varies greatly among women, and all sizes and shapes are normal and healthy."

www.teengrowth.com

Some girls enjoy choosing a first bra. Others feel shy or embarrassed, so may get their parents to choose them.

MONTHLY CYCLE

A girl's monthly cycle begins on the first day of her period and runs through to the day before her next period. The average cycle is around 28 days, but anything between 22 and 35 days is considered normal. Periods can be irregular in the first few months, and again later in a woman's life during the **menopause** (around the early fifties) when the monthly cycle ceases.

What are periods?

Periods normally begin about two years after the start of puberty. The average age is 12, but they can start at any age between 8 and 16.

A baby girl is born with around 500,000 eggs stored in follicles (sacs) in her ovaries. The eggs mature when her body begins to produce sex hormones.

If you are a girl, once puberty starts, your body releases an egg every month from your ovaries. This is called ovulation. The egg travels down the fallopian tubes to the uterus (womb). The lining of the uterus thickens so it is ready for a baby to grow if the egg is fertilized by male **sperm**. If it is not fertilized, the egg and the soft lining of the uterus are shed as blood and other material through the vagina when you have your "period."

This illustration shows the 28-day menstrual cycle.

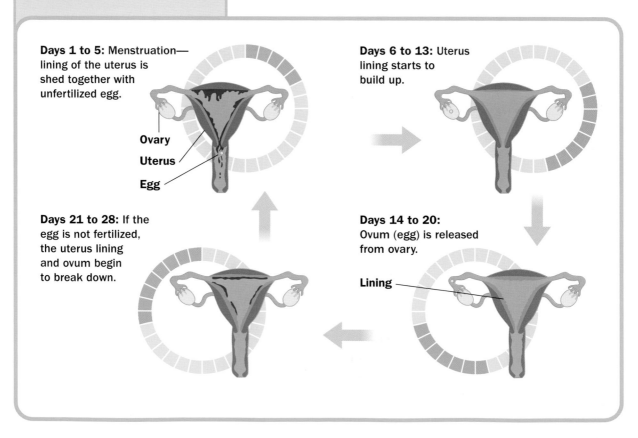

Days 1 to 5: Menstruation—lining of the uterus is shed together with unfertilized egg.

Ovary
Uterus
Egg

Days 6 to 13: Uterus lining starts to build up.

Days 21 to 28: If the egg is not fertilized, the uterus lining and ovum begin to break down.

Days 14 to 20: Ovum (egg) is released from ovary.

Lining

On average, periods last about five days, but they can vary from one to eight days, especially during the first few months. Only a small amount of blood, an average of around 1.35 ounces (40 ml), is lost during a period, and normally flow is heaviest in the first couple of days. You may experience stomach pains, or cramps, at the start of your period. This is because the uterus is contracting or squeezing to release the egg and soft lining.

PMS

Premenstrual syndrome, or PMS, is the name for some of the symptoms that can occur in the days leading up to a period. They include feeling bloated (as the changing levels of estrogen cause the body to retain more water), tender and swollen breasts, nausea, headaches, and feeling tearful, irritable, and tired. Some girls find they have a craving for sweet foods.

Tampons are made of soft cotton pressed together to form a cylinder-like shape, so that they can be easily inserted.

Can I use tampons?

Dear Agony Aunt,
My periods have just started, and I really want to use tampons, but when I tried, I just had to give up. I think my vagina may just be too small. Is that possible?
Amy, 12

Dear Amy,
It can be hard the first few times, but it is not because your vagina is too small or tight. After all, it is capable of stretching enough for a baby to get through! When you become tense, the vagina tightens so it is important to relax when you are inserting a tampon. Choose one of the smaller "mini" tampons to start with. Try raising one leg on a chair and relax by taking some deep breaths. If this still doesn't work, you can use other sanitary products. You may also want to visit your doctor if you are still worried.

FAQ

3 Body changes: boys

Boys can begin puberty any time between the ages of around 9 and 15. Hormones start working on the **testes** so they begin to produce sperm, and on the adrenal glands so they produce androgens (male sex hormones), chiefly **testosterone**.

First signs

If you are a boy, you will have a sudden growth spurt, and your body will change shape, getting stronger and more muscular. Your skeleton can grow up to a third of an inch (1 cm) a month during puberty. Your shoulders get wider, and muscles in your neck, chest, and legs grow bigger and stronger as testosterone makes the muscle fibers multiply and thicken.

Having personal space becomes increasingly important during the teen years.

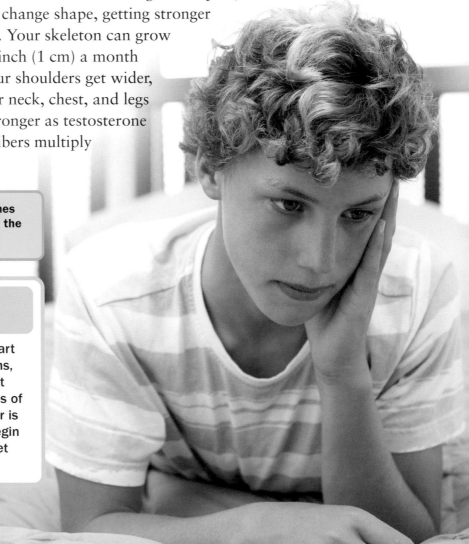

WHEN DOES SHAVING START?

Most boys don't need to start shaving until their late teens, but they can decide to start anywhere between the ages of around 13 and 19. The hair is often fine and patchy to begin with, but it will gradually get thicker and coarser.

Hanging out with friends is part of gaining independence away from the family.

WHY DO BOYS' VOICES BREAK?

Before puberty, your larynx is fairly small, and your vocal cords are small and thin. That's why your voice is higher than an adult's. During puberty, the larynx gets bigger, and the vocal cords lengthen and thicken, making your voice deeper. Part of the larynx can become visible as the "Adam's apple" in your throat. As the body adjusts to this change, your voice may "crack" or "break." This process should last for only a few months.

Skin and hair become more oily and the sweat glands become more active and begin to produce a different kind of sweat (see page 24). Body hair begins to grow on the face, underarms, legs, chest, belly, and around the pubic area. Some boys go on growing more body hair into their twenties, and they may want to start shaving facial hair and shaving or waxing unwanted body hair.

As sex hormones start to work, the **penis** and testes increase in size. The penis is the fastest-growing part of a boy's body during puberty. It gets longer and thicker and also becomes highly sensitive to touch. The **testicles** also grow up to seven times their original size, often one slightly faster than the other.

Voice breaking

Another sign of puberty is that your voice begins to "break," becoming deeper. This typically happens between the ages of around 11 and 14, after the main "growth spurt."

WHAT CAUSES "MAN BOOBS"?

Experts believe a temporary imbalance in androgens and estrogens—the hormones that kick in during puberty—can cause a temporary growth in breast tissue (gynecomastia). It affects about 50 percent of boys, and in most cases only lasts a few months.

HEALTH WARNING

Alcohol and some drugs can stimulate male breast growth. These drugs include body-building steroids, amphetamines, marijuana, and heroin. These drugs also have other very serious side effects and should be avoided wherever possible.

Comparing yourself to others, for example, friends or celebrities, is natural during puberty.

Is it normal?

Boys develop at different rates during puberty, and this means they may worry that they are not normal when they compare themselves with classmates.

Penis size

Boys often worry that although the testes are growing, their penis is not growing big or fast enough. Normal adult penis size covers a wide range and varies more when soft or flaccid, around 2 to 4 inches (5–10 cm), than when erect at around 5 to 6 inches (13–16 cm). It can take until you are around 19 or 20 for your penis to reach its full size. You may also worry about changes in the scrotum, but the skin naturally becomes darker during puberty and also becomes rougher in texture before body hair grows.

Am I normal?

If you look at pictures in magazines and on the Internet, you may find yourself comparing your own body to these, worrying that you don't match up. You may worry that your erection (see page 18) is abnormal, for example, because it has a bend or curve when erect. There are many variations in how erections look, and all are normal, but if you have any concerns, you can always ask your doctor, who will be able to reassure you.

Body checks

Some doctors recommend that boys should check their testes for any changes or lumps from the age of around 15 years. Getting to know the normal feel of their scrotum and testes will help boys be aware of any changes that could indicate problems including testicular cancer. Some teenage boys may develop a twisted testicle which can cause pain, redness, and swelling, and this should always be checked out by a doctor immediately.

Boys (and men) can sometimes find it harder to talk about problems than females do.

Am I turning into a girl?

Dear Agony Aunt,
I am really worried because I think I am growing breasts. My friends started teasing me at the pool last week, and now I don't want to go swimming any more. What's happening? I am worried something is wrong with me, and I am turning into a girl. I'm quite thin, so I know it can't be related to weight gain.
Chris, 14

Dear Chris,
Don't worry. You are not changing into a girl. In puberty, normal changes in hormone levels can make a boy's breasts begin to swell under the nipples. It can happen on one or both sides, and they may feel a bit tender, too. Usually, they will flatten out in a few months or at most a year or two. They are not related to body weight.

WHAT CAUSES AN ERECTION?

The penis is made of spongy tissue filled with tiny blood vessels. Normally blood flows in and out of the penis at the same rate, but during an erection, blood vessels at the base of the penis tighten and blood flow increases dramatically into the penis, making it get bigger and harder.

IT HAPPENED TO ME

I got my first wet dream when I was at a friend's sleepover. I was really embarrassed because, when I woke up, my boxers and the sleeping bag were damp, and I thought I had wet the bed. Luckily I managed to hide it from my friend.

Darren, 15

Erections

Erections are when a boy's penis fills with blood so that it becomes larger and stiffer, standing up against the body. During an erection, a penis grows up to five times its normal size. Boys can have erections when they are babies or children, but during puberty, it starts to happen more often.

Arousal or reflex

If you are a boy, you can have an erection when you are turned on by sexual thoughts or looking at someone you find attractive and sexy. Erections can make you feel embarrassed, and during puberty, they can often happen spontaneously. Teenage boys can have up to 20 "reflex" erections a day. They can sometimes feel embarrassed when it happens like this, but mostly no one else will notice, and thinking about something nonsexual can help make it go down.

Wet dreams

Most teenage boys have about four erections during the night while they are sleeping. Some can result in a wet dream, which is when you **ejaculate semen** in your sleep. Wet dreams are normal and natural; they are nothing to feel embarrassed about.

Ejaculation

When a boy reaches **orgasm**—whether through **masturbation** (see page 28), sex, or wet dreams—the penis releases a spurt of semen, the fluid that carries sperm. Each ejaculation can carry up to 100 million sperm. Sperm can fertilize a female egg during sex to produce a baby.

Wet dreams are most common during adolescence and early young adult years. However, they may happen any time during or after puberty.

FAQ

4 Skin and hair

The hormones that bring about body changes in puberty also affect the skin and hair. The skin contains thousands of microscopic **sebaceous** glands that produce sebum (an oily substance) to stop skin and hair drying out. But in puberty, too much sebum can build up, making the skin and hair look and feel oily. This oil can lead to blackheads and pimples.

As we reach puberty, the male sex hormones, androgens, cause the sebaceous glands to enlarge and produce more sebum. Both boys and girls have some male and some female sex hormones, but boys have around ten times more testosterone than girls, and girls have around ten times more estrogen than boys.

WORSE FOR BOYS?

As boys have more androgens than girls do, they can suffer more with greasy skin and hair. In girls, estrogen keeps the production of sebum down, but girls do have small amounts of testosterone. If this is not countered by enough estrogen (for example, estrogen levels drop just before girls' periods) their skin can become more greasy and prone to pimples.

Keep it clean!

Acne is not caused by dirty skin. Too much sebum can block skin **pores**, leading to pimples and acne (see page 22). Sebum can also build up around the hair follicles, making the hair look greasy and lank soon after washing. You can help by keeping your skin and hair clean with gentle washing—but washing your face more than twice a day can stimulate more oil to be produced. Use noncomedogenic skin products (this means they won't block the pores). There are lots of products designed especially for oily skin and hair, and it is worth experimenting to see which work best for you. Pimples nearly always disappear after puberty.

Acne is worse premenstrually—many girls notice their pimples are worse during the week before a period.

Can I prevent pimples?

Dear Agony Aunt,
My skin feels really greasy, and I get pimples especially around my period. They make me really self-conscious, and I seem to get them much more than anyone else. Is there anything I can do to prevent them?
Beatriz, 15

Dear Beatriz,
Pimples are generally a result of excessively oily skin. Find a face wash designed for oily skin, as this will help to control the amount of oils that are being secreted on to the surface of the skin. You can also buy facial strips that have been designed to help get rid of blackheads. For the best results, you should use these when your skin is clean and soft—perhaps after a bath or shower. Remember that what works for someone else may not work for you, so you may need to experiment in finding a product that is suitable for your skin.

"Acne is the most common skin disorder in the United States, affecting 40 million to 50 million Americans . . . By mid-teens, more than 40 percent of adolescents have acne or acne scarring, which requires treatment by a dermatologist."

American Academy of Dermatology

HEALTH WARNING

When pimples appear, it can be tempting to squeeze them, especially if there is a "head" and you can see fatty matter inside. But this can cause a pimple to become infected with bacteria from the skin, fingers, or nails, leading to more inflammation and scarring.

PROBLEM SKIN: ACNE
What is acne?

We all have thousands of microscopic **bacteria** living on our skin and in our hair. The bacteria feed on the sebum produced by the sebaceous glands. As they feed, bacteria thicken the sebum. If too much is being produced, it can begin to block the skin pores causing whiteheads, blackheads, pimples, and **cysts**. Acne occurs when these blocked pores become infected and inflamed. It can occur on the face, neck, back, and sometimes the chest.

Genes (as they affect the skin type you inherit from your parents), stress and, for girls, the time around their monthly period, can all contribute to acne outbreaks.

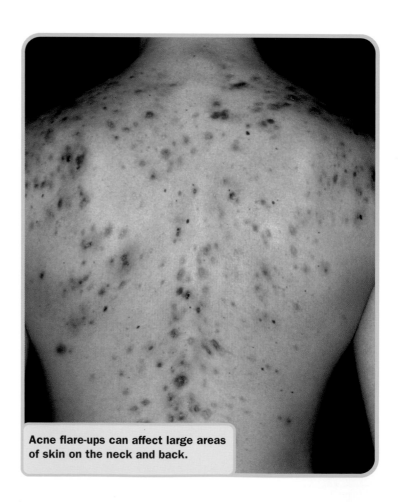

Acne flare-ups can affect large areas of skin on the neck and back.

Medication can sometimes help to control severe acne.

Not just physical

Acne pimples can become so inflamed that they can lead to permanent scarring. They can also feel sore and tender to touch. Acne is not just a physical problem; it can lead to low self-esteem (see page 42), lack of social confidence and can even affect everyday life, for example, stifling a social life or causing truancy from school.

Treatments

Keep bacteria at bay by gentle washing of your skin. There are over-the-counter products (facial washes, creams, and gels) which may help. However, if these do not work after six to eight weeks of use, it is worth consulting a doctor. Doctors can prescribe medications in cream or tablet form that work either by reducing the amount of sebum produced by the sebaceous glands or by controlling the bacteria on the skin that can lead to acne. It can be a few weeks before you see the results. For severe cases, doctors may refer patients for laser therapy or **dermabrasion**, which can help reduce scarring.

SWEATING: WHY IS IT SUDDENLY A PROBLEM?
What is sweat?

Sweat is made mostly from water and salts and is our body's way of cooling us down. Sweat glands in the skin produce a watery fluid that has a cooling effect as it evaporates on our skin. One kind of sweat gland, the eccrine glands, are found all over the body, but in puberty another kind of sweat gland starts working.

A new kind of sweat

As we reach puberty, the aprocrine glands begin producing a different kind of sweat that contains oils. These glands are especially concentrated around the **groin** area, under the arms and on our feet. They produce sweat at the same time as the eccrine glands—for example when you get hot because of warm weather or when you have been rushing around or exercising, and also when you become stressed.

Why does it smell?

Sweat only begins to smell and cause the unpleasant odors we call body odor (B.O.) when the bacteria living on our skin and clothes begin to break it down to produce the fatty acids they feed on. We tend to get more of these bacteria on and around the groin, armpits, and

Do I smell?

Dear Agony Aunt,
I sweat so much that sometimes I feel too embarrassed to take my jacket off because of the sweat patches under my arms. I am also really worried that I might smell because of it. What can I do?
Sam, 14

Dear Sam,
Lots of teenagers suffer from sweat and body odor problems, so you're not alone. There are some things that you can do to try to reduce the amount that you sweat. Make sure you have a bath or shower once a day. Try applying an antiperspirant deodorant after a shower and take it with you to school, in case you need to apply some more throughout the day. You could also carry some wet wipes in your bag, so that you can have a quick wash at lunchtime, before applying more antiperspirant. To avoid odor, remember to change your underwear and socks every day, and your clothes before they start to smell. Don't wear the same shoes every day. Finally, avoid eating too many strong-flavored foods (onions, garlic, spicy foods) as they can make sweat smell more.

feet as they produce most of the oily kind of sweat. If not kept under control by washing and changing our clothes, the bacteria have time to grow and multiply as they feed, making the smell get stronger (as with athletic shoes worn day after day).

Keep it in check

Daily showering, focusing particularly on the armpits, face, feet, and **genitals**, will help to stop sweat becoming stale and smelly. Once puberty starts, most young people choose to start using an underarm deodorant or antiperspirant. These come in many forms (as sticks, roll-ons, and sprays).

HOW DO DEODORANTS WORK?

Deodorants contain fragrances to mask bad smells and ingredients such as alcohol and antimicrobials to kill bacteria. Antiperspirants contain aluminum salts that dissolve in sweat. They then coat the skin in a fine gel that covers the sweat glands and reduces the amount of sweat they produce.

Underarm deodorants or antiperspirants should be part of a daily hygiene routine.

FAQ

5 Emotions

Mood swings

The hormones that become active during puberty don't just cause physical changes. They also affect the way you feel. It is normal to have frequent mood swings during puberty. This is due to a temporary imbalance in hormone levels, and it will settle down. However, it is important to remember that your feelings are no less valid, or real, for being caused by hormones.

Cooling-off time can help you calm down and avoid arguments.

Coping with feelings

Hormonal swings mean you can feel irritable and angry one minute and be laughing and happy the next. You can also seesaw between bursts of energy and feeling really tired and sleepy. This can be the result of all the growing you are doing, along with other physical changes your body is going through. Sudden changes in energy levels can affect your mood, too.

Relaxation

Eating healthily and getting plenty of exercise and sleep during puberty, can all help to counter mood swings. You can also practice relaxation techniques such as counting to ten or taking slow, deep breaths when you feel anger building up. Keeping active and doing a hobby you love are effective ways of lifting your mood.

BRAIN CHANGES

It is not only hormones in puberty that cause mood swings. The brain is changing and growing just as the body is. Scientists believe that the last part of the brain to mature is the frontal lobe, the part responsible for self-control, judgment, and decision making. This makes teens more likely to behave in an impulsive or even reckless way and to have less control over powerful feelings. During puberty, you can feel emotions very intensely, whether it be anger, love, or sadness.

How can I control my anger?

Dear Agony Aunt,
I seem to fight all the time with my mom. It's over the most stupid things, like whether I've remembered to put my dirty washing in the basket. It drives me mad. I end up shouting awful things and then feeling bad about it. I can't seem to stop myself!
Katy, 13

Dear Katy,
I'm sorry to hear you are arguing lots with your mom. Most teenagers experience this, but there are some small things you can do to try to change things. When you feel yourself about to snap, force yourself to take some deep breaths before you speak. Try not to shout or scream and try to make "I" rather than "you" statements. Say "I am always being told off," rather than "You always tell me off." You could also try to write things down in a diary, instead of having an argument. Go to your room and write it all down. This will help you calm down, and you'll be able to reflect on your feelings afterward. Finally, remember that your mom is probably only trying to help and may be a little stressed herself. For example, she may be fussing about the washing because she is feeling stressed about keeping the house running smoothly.

WHAT IS SEX DRIVE?

Sex drive—the desire to have sex—is produced by the sex hormone testosterone. In females, sex drive is created by small amounts of testosterone produced by the ovaries and adrenal glands. Rising levels of testosterone in puberty make boys more competitive and aggressive, as well as creating the libido or desire for sex.

THE M WORD

There are lots of myths about masturbation: that if you do it too much it can make your hands hairy or make you go blind or that it is only normal for boys to do it. In fact it is common for both boys and girls to masturbate and is in no way harmful to your body. However, not all teenagers do, and this is just as normal.

Sexual awareness

Puberty prepares your body for having sex and reproducing. When your body begins producing sex hormones during puberty, it is natural to start having sexual thoughts and feelings.

Arousal

You may have sexual thoughts toward or about others. You may think about them almost constantly and have fantasies where you imagine being with them. As well as sexual thoughts, you may begin to feel physically aroused when you look at sexy images or when you are close to people who attract you. Arousal in boys can result in erections. Girls may experience symptoms of arousal such as an increased heart rate, blushing, and increased wetness in the vagina.

Masturbation

You may become aware that touching sensitive areas of your body feels pleasurable. Touching, stroking, or rubbing sexual parts for pleasure (for boys the penis, and for girls the **clitoris** and nipples) is called masturbation. For many teenagers, it is a way of getting to know their bodies as they mature sexually.

"The average age that an adolescent begins to masturbate is eleven years, eight months. Forty-five percent of males and fifteen percent of females masturbate before age thirteen."

Western Michigan University, USA

Mixing with peers of both sexes can naturally lead to feelings of attraction among teens.

Sexuality

As you begin to have sexual thoughts and fantasies, you will discover your own sexuality. Sexuality is awareness of you as a sexual being, and also awareness of sexual attraction to others. Some people are heterosexual (attracted to people of the opposite sex). Others are homosexual (attracted to people of the same sex). Some are bisexual (attracted to people of both sexes).

Flirting is part of establishing your sexuality and learning to interact with others.

Being gay

Some teenagers are very sure at an early stage that they are homosexual or gay. Others may experience feelings of attraction to both boys and girls before working out their feelings. Some young people who are gay find it hard to acknowledge their feelings to themselves, let alone to others. This may lead to someone feeling worried and alone in coping with his or her emotions. Keeping sexuality a secret is not something that is healthy or workable in the long run, and it will help if you can find someone you trust, whom you can confide in and explain how you are feeling.

"Gay teenagers are 'coming out' earlier than ever, and many feel better about themselves than earlier generations of gays."

USATODAY.com

IT HAPPENED TO ME

When I realized I had feelings toward other boys, I felt I was carrying around this huge secret. My dad has no time for gay people so it was mom I turned to. I can honestly say worrying about telling them was worse than doing it because mom made me realize it wasn't something I had done; it was just how things are. She helped me talk to Dad about it, too, and though it was a difficult conversation, he is now beginning to accept it.

Gabriel, 17

Am I gay?

Dear Agony Aunt,
I'm a 13-year-old girl, and I have a crush on an older girl at school. I can't stop thinking about her. When she talks to me, I get really embarrassed but feel excited afterward. Does this mean I am gay?
Shona, 13

Dear Shona,
It is very normal to have a crush on someone of the same sex when you are growing up, but it doesn't mean you are necessarily gay. Girls often have crushes on older female pupils, teachers, or pop stars. In puberty, as you search around for role models, you may find yourself looking up to someone, wanting to be like them, and feeling a bit in love with them, all at the same time. Most crushes like yours are not indicators of sexuality. However, it depends on how you are feeling. If you have had these kinds of feelings for other girls in the past, or if you go on to have persistent feelings toward girls or women in the future, then it might mean you are more attracted to girls than boys. The important thing to remember is that these feelings would be normal for you, and they are nothing to be ashamed about.

FAQ

6 Your body

Body weight

All boys and girls put on weight during puberty as a normal part of growing. The weight gain in puberty comes from an increase in fat, muscle, bone, and body tissue. Weight and height gain can be uneven, so that some young people grow in height as their body weight increases, while others will put on weight just before a growth spurt. Weight gain in puberty is sometimes called "baby fat."

HEALTH WARNING

All the growing you do in puberty can give you a big appetite, but it is important to balance your **calorie** intake with activity and exercise. **Obesity** carries many health risks including asthma and type **2 diabetes**, and increased risk of heart disease and high blood pressure. Individuals who are obese have a 50 to 100 percent increased risk of premature death from all causes, compared to individuals with a healthy weight.

BMI

Doctors use body mass index (BMI) to assess whether someone is underweight, a healthy weight, or overweight. For adults, BMI is calculated by dividing their weight in pounds, multiplied by 703, by the square of their height in inches. For young people, doctors compare height and weight against statistics for others of the same age and then rank them according to percentiles. Someone who is in the 60th percentile for height is taller than 60 percent of others in their age range, and shorter than 40 percent of others. There are separate BMI charts for boys and girls and for weight and height. Health experts recommend a BMI for adults between 18.5 and 25.

Balanced diet

To grow and stay healthy, your body needs energy (measured in calories or **kilojoules**) which is provided by food. A healthy diet contains foods from each of the four main food groups, which are:

- starchy carbohydrates (bread, cereals, and potatoes)
- fresh fruit and vegetables
- milk and dairy foods
- meat, fish, and legumes.

Vitamins and minerals (found in fresh fruits and vegetables) are especially important while you are growing. Foods that are high in saturated fats or sugars (cakes, cookies, chips) should be eaten only occasionally as they have little nutritional value and can lead to too much fat being stored in your body. Eating too many foods containing fats and sugars, along with lack of exercise, can cause young people to become overweight or even obese.

Recommended daily calories

Age	Girls	Boys
7–10	1740	1970
11–14	1845	2220
15–18	2110	2755

Those who are very active may need more calories, and those who are very inactive and do little exercise may require fewer.

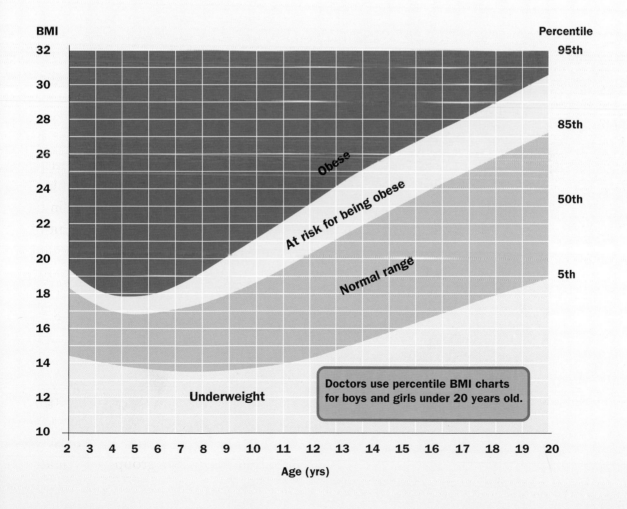

BMI | Percentile

Obese

At risk for being obese

Normal range

Underweight

Doctors use percentile BMI charts for boys and girls under 20 years old.

Age (yrs)

SIZE ZERO

The fashion industry has been criticized for promoting "size zero" models. These models with a U.S. 0 clothes size (a U.K. size 4) often have a BMI that falls below the recommended healthy range (between 18.5 and 25).

Magazines can bombard us with idealized images that set impossible standards.

Body image

Body image is how we see ourselves. It is influenced by many factors. This can include things people say about us, or comparisons of ourselves to others (such as our peers), or to images we see in the media. Our body image can be very different from the actual shape and appearance of our bodies.

Most of us have something we would like to change about the way we look. But some people can have such a poor or negative body image that it affects their self-esteem (see page 42) and their well-being.

Media influences

During puberty, you can feel unsure of how you are meant to look as your body changes in significant ways. You can begin to feel self-conscious and become sensitive about personal remarks (such as comments about your weight or your acne). You may compare yourself to images you see in the media and feel upset or depressed if you feel you don't measure up.

Images of celebrities are regularly airbrushed to achieve the appearance of flawless skin and a perfect body shape. Some advertising campaigns use body part models who model just hands, or feet, or legs, and these are then digitally assembled to create a perfect model who is not a real person at all. All these enhancements make girls, women, boys, and men feel inferior when they compare themselves against the perfect ideal and can lead to negative body image or even body dysmorphia (a disorder in which people become obsessed with what they see as flaws in their body or body shape).

Poor body image has been blamed as a factor in the increasing numbers of **eating disorders** (see page

36) in young people. It can also lead to dieting unnecessarily. Unless your BMI shows that you are much heavier than others in your peer group, dieting is not recommended while your body is growing, as you need a balanced diet at this time (see page 8 for other health risks).

Many fashion models have a BMI that is well below the recommended healthy range.

IT HAPPENED TO ME

For years I've read celebrity magazines full of super-slim, gorgeous people and thought, "I want to look like that." The magazines poke fun at people when they put on weight. Two years ago, I started dieting to look like them. But recently I got worried because my periods hadn't started. My doctor explained it could be because I was seriously underweight. I gave up dieting, and it was such a relief when my periods started recently.

Tamsin, 14

FAQ

7 Your health

Eating disorders

Eating disorders can begin at any time in life, but often they start in puberty or the early teens. Eating disorders are not just about food and weight; they're also about the way someone feels inside. Food becomes a problem when it is used to help people cope with difficult situations or feelings.

Who gets eating disorders?

People who develop eating disorders may be high achievers and may have issues with self-esteem. They can be perfectionists who try to do everything well and criticize or blame themselves for what they see as failures. They can also become obsessive, so, in their minds, food and weight become the main focus, and they think about them all the time. Eating disorders are most common among girls, but significant numbers of boys have eating disorders, too.

There are three main types of eating disorder.

Anorexia nervosa

People with anorexia have an intense fear of weight gain. Even when they are terribly underweight and skinny, they see themselves as fat. They try to control the amount they eat by skipping meals and eating very little or by making themselves sick if they feel they have eaten too much. They think about food and calories a lot and may weigh themselves very frequently.

Binge eating

Binge eating disorder is when someone eats huge amounts of food in a short space of time. Often they choose foods like chocolate bars or ice cream and then feel guilty and ashamed about bingeing. Binge eating can lead to someone becoming overweight or obese.

Bulimia nervosa

People with bulimia nervosa also think constantly about food, but they get into a cycle of binge eating, before **purging**, either by making themselves sick or by taking **laxatives**. Often they will feel guilty and ashamed after bingeing, but the purging alters their mood so they

An anorexic may push the food around their plate rather than eating it. They might also make excuses to take the food to their room, where they will dispose of it.

"It is estimated that there is one man for every 20 women with anorexia. The estimate is that there is one man for every 10 women with bulimia."

National Eating Disorder Information Center, Canada

IT HAPPENED TO ME

When I was 13, I started putting on weight. It didn't feel right and when the P.E. teacher teased me for being a bit chubby, I decided to go on a diet. At first I just skipped breakfast and threw my lunch away. My friends said I was looking slimmer and that made me diet even more. I started hiding what I was doing. I think that was when it got bad, and I started to need help. Eventually my mom noticed and persuaded me to see my doctor. I'm now trying to eat a balanced, healthy diet and not obsess about weight so much.

Jessica, 14

can feel calm or happy, as if they are back in control again. Some do this occasionally, when they are under stress; for others, it is regular or even daily behavior.

Eating disorders can be serious and dangerous or even life-threatening if not treated. Severe weight loss and lack of proper nutrition cause health problems including stunted growth, brittle bones, and a weak **immune system**. In girls, monthly periods may stop altogether.

Treatments

Experts believe that eating disorders are often a way of getting control over one area of life (weight gain) when everything else feels out of control. Treatments include nutrition; counseling, especially focusing on self-esteem (see page 42); and, in more serious cases, a stay in a specialist clinic or hospital.

Adolescence and mental health
Some young people experience different forms of behavior disorders, such as anxiety disorder, or more rarely, obsessive compulsive disorder (OCD), and bipolar disorder. Some of these may appear at the same time as eating disorders.

Anxiety disorder
Anxiety often occurs without a particular trigger. A certain amount of anxiety may be a normal reaction to stress. It may help a person to deal with a difficult situation—for example, exams at school—by prompting him or her to cope with it. When anxiety becomes excessive, it is an anxiety disorder.

Anxiety disorder affects young people by making them feel fearful or worried all of the time. They often miss school because of physical symptoms, such as frequent headaches and stomach aches. Inside, they may be constantly worried, either generally or by something in particular such as the fear of being separated from parents or fear about developing friendships at school.

OCD
OCD takes many different forms, but it usually involves obsessive thoughts or behavior, such as washing hands compulsively or putting things into a strict tidy order. When someone has OCD, they feel they must perform these "rituals" to stop bad things from happening. It is important to try and break the cycle because thinking about or performing repetitive rituals makes the OCD stronger. Resisting—however hard—weakens it.

Bipolar disorder
Bipolar disorder, also known as manic-depressive disorder, is usually indicated by someone having very extreme moods. They can appear manically overexcited or, in contrast, very

The upheavals of puberty involve changes in the brain that may contribute to behavior disorders.

Why do I feel so anxious?

Dear Agony Aunt,
Lately I've been feeling really anxious and stressed, and I don't know why. It's not about anything in particular. I have trouble sleeping at night, and when I do, I have nightmares. My heart pounds at the smallest thing, and I feel like something terrible is going to happen. I can't concentrate at school, and I keep snapping at my friends. How can I feel less anxious when I don't even know what I'm anxious about?
Cristian, 14

Dear Cristian,
Anxiety can affect your day-to-day life and be very upsetting. However, there are ways to deal with it. Look at your diet and exercise—healthy foods, regular meals, and exercise will improve your overall health and well-being. Find relaxation techniques—for example, you could go for a walk, listen to some favorite music, or play football with a friend. Talk to someone about your feelings and see if you can find a solution. Think positive—you may find it hard at first, but try it for just a few days, and you will find yourself not only more relaxed, but perhaps even more energetic. Hopefully these tips can help ease some of your stress. If you continue to suffer from serious anxiety, you should consider visiting your doctor, who may recommend counseling or medication.

depressed; they may even show symptoms of both at once. These episodes are usually separated by "normal" moods. Extreme manic episodes can sometimes lead to symptoms such as delusions and hallucinations.

Bipolar disorder usually starts in adolescence or early adulthood, particularly for girls. Boys are more prone than girls to develop bipolar disorder before puberty, but also develop it as teenagers.

Treatment for all these kinds of disorders is often counseling, which aims to get to the root causes of the problem. But in some cases, doctors may prescribe medications which can help those with the disorders to get through difficult times.

"Puberty may have an impact on areas of the brain that contribute to bipolar disorder or schizophrenia in youth, according to a study . . . The findings add to the evidence that adolescence is a critical period of vulnerability for the development of schizophrenia and bipolar disorder."

Science Daily,
December 10, 2007

Bottling up painful feelings can lead to sickness, but support can help you through difficult times.

IT HAPPENED TO ME

When I was 12, we moved, and I found it hard to make new friends. Then I started getting bullied at school. I got more and more depressed. In the end, I confided in my teacher. He told me about a mental health project where I could meet and talk to other young people who are going through the same sort of problems as me. We do things like art and media filming and sometimes we just chat about how we are feeling. It really has helped me to talk to people and I've made some good friends, too.

Nicolas, 14

Stress and depression

Feeling low some of the time is normal, especially during puberty, when hormones are affecting not just your body but also the way you feel. However, although it's normal to feel down some of the time, you shouldn't have to feel down all the time—and if you do, you should seek help from others.

Coping with problems

As you approach your teens, it is normal to start wanting more control over your own life, yet things are happening to you that you can't change or stop. Events can also make you feel you have no say over your life. For example, imagine that your parents divorce and the family is split up or that you lose someone close to you, such as a grandparent, through a death. Problems with friends, bullying, and any form of abuse (which means someone is behaving toward you in ways that make you uncomfortable or unhappy) can also affect your self-esteem and well-being (see page 42). Even without these problems, all the changes you go through as you move from being a young person to an adult can be stressful and make you feel confused about who you are or that you are not "good enough." Feeling we are not in control of what happens to us—at any stage in our life—can make us feel insecure and unhappy.

Depression

If you feel low all of the time during puberty, you may have depression. People who are depressed often feel unhappy, have no interest or energy, suffer sleep problems, and withdraw from others. The way they feel starts interfering with their everyday lives, stopping them from doing things that they might otherwise do because they lose interest or just feel too tired. They may feel so low that they start to have thoughts about **self-harming** or even suicide.

If you think you may be depressed, it is important to see your doctor. He or she can get help for you, either through medication or counseling. Never bottle up feelings of depression: talking about them to someone you trust—whether a relative, school nurse, counselor, doctor, or youth worker—is the first step to feeling better.

Teenage boys and young men are a high-risk group for depression.

Being you

Puberty doesn't just mean that your body is changing; you are growing as a person, too. You are likely to start wanting to become more independent. You also may want to rebel against parents, teachers and others in authority to show them that you have your own ideas and opinions and can also make your own choices. Some days you may be brimming with confidence and other days feel unsure of who you are or what you want to do with your life.

Self-esteem

We all need to develop our self-esteem. This means that we value ourselves all the time and not just when we get good marks in a test, are looking slim, or are showing off our "coolest" clothes or possessions. It means having realistic expectations of yourself, praising yourself when you put in effort and do something well, and making allowances when you make mistakes or experience failure or rejection.

Dance is a great way of expressing yourself and making the most of being young.

Should I join in?

Dear Agony Aunt,
The crowd I got in with at my new school all drink alcohol when they are hanging out after school, even though we are only 15. They keep offering it to me, and when I say "No," they just laugh at me and call me a lightweight. I am worried that they won't want me to be in the gang any more if I don't join in. What do I tell them?
Danyl, 15

Dear Danyl,
As you go through puberty, if friends no longer want your company just because you won't act the same as they do, they are not really friends in the first place. Making you do something you don't feel comfortable with is a form of bullying, however subtle. Shrug off the name-calling and tell them that you can make your own decisions. Remember that you will be happier if you don't let yourself be pushed around.

Peer pressure

Peer pressure can be a strong influence during puberty. Your peers can put pressure on you to behave in a certain way, such as taking up smoking or drinking alcohol. They can also make fun of you or make you feel bad if you are not keeping up with the latest clothes, gadgets, or other possessions. You may feel worried that if you don't join in, they will see you as "uncool" or childish. But it is important to realize that making a stand for yourself, and not just going along with the crowd and seeking their approval, is far more mature and shows that you have self-esteem.

Taking part in group activities can be a good way of building self-esteem.

Puberty involves lots of changes. Ups and downs are a normal part of it and will pass. All of this is part of the process of reaching young adulthood, which brings greater freedoms and responsibilities, and new choices.

Glossary

adrenal glands a pair of glands just above the kidneys that produce hormones

anemia a condition in which not enough oxygen is carried in the blood due to a lack of red blood cells. It can make you tired, faint, and breathless.

bacteria tiny living organisms

calories (kilo calories/kilojoules) the measure of energy in food or drink

clitoris small highly sensitive part of the female vulva between the labia minora

cyst a closed sac having a distinct membrane that keeps it separate from nearby tissue

depression condition of long-term emotional dejection and withdrawal

dermabrasion a surgical procedure that uses abrasives to remove scarring and other skin imperfections

diabetes a condition in which the body is unable to regulate the level of sugar in the blood

eating disorder a damaged or inappropriate relationship with food, resulting in a failure to eat healthily

ejaculate to release semen

estrogen female sex hormone

genes the units of heredity by which characteristics pass from parent to child

genitals sexual organs

groin the area where the upper thighs meet the trunk of the body, including the external genitals

heredity the passing on of genetic characteristics from one generation to the next

immune system the body's natural defenses against illnesses and disease

kilojoule a unit of energy equal to 1,000 joules—4,184 joules is equivalent to one food calorie

labia the liplike external female genitalia (the labia majora and labia minora)

laxatives medicines that stimulate the bowels

masturbation touching your own sexual parts for pleasure

menopause time in a woman's life when her monthly periods cease completely

menstruation the bleeding that follows the breakdown of the lining of the uterus every four weeks if the egg produced by the ovaries remains unfertilized

obese severely overweight, for adults a BMI of 30 or above

obesity state of being severely overweight

orgasm sexual climax that brings intense pleasure

ovaries female reproductive organs that produce eggs

penis male reproductive organ

pore any tiny hole in the skin admitting passage of a liquid

progesterone female sex hormone

purging getting rid of; cleansing

reproduction creating babies

schizophrenia a serious mental disorder in which people can lose touch with reality. People can have hallucinations and delusions; they may feel paranoid and muddled and have difficulty concentrating.

scrotum pouch or sack of skin that contains the testes

sebaceous secreting sebum or oil

self-harming deliberately harming oneself (such as cutting or burning the skin)

semen the whitish fluid that carries sperm

sperm male reproductive cell carried in semen

testes/testicles male reproductive glands

testosterone male sex hormone

vagina passage leading from the vulva to the uterus (womb)

vulva the female external genital organs including the labia majora, labia minora, clitoris, and the entrance to the vagina

Further information

WEB SITES

www.anad.org
Web site of the National Association of Anorexia and Associated Eating Disorders.

www.teenhelp.org
This web site is run by an international not-for-profit organisation, and offers various different ways for teens to get advice and support.

www.cyh.com
Comprehensive web site with kids and teens sections providing information on puberty by the Australian Child and Youth Health Service.

www.kidshealth.org, and www.teenshealth.com
These web sites are part of the series of web sites—for kids, teens, and parents—run by the nonprofit Nemours Center for Children's Health Media. One of the sites' goals is to give visitors up-to-date information on growth and health issues.

BOOKS

Kelli Dunham, *The Boys' Body Book: Everything You Need to Know for Growing Up You*, Applesauce Press, 2007

Kelli Dunham, *The Girls' Body Book: Everything You Need to Know for Growing Up You*, Applesauce Press, 2007

Elinor Greenwood, *100% Me*, Dorling Kindersley, 2008

Elisabeth Henderson and Dr. Nancy Armstrong, *100 Questions You'd Never Ask Your Parents*, Uppman Publishing, 2007

Index

alcohol 16, 43
antiperspirant 8, 24–25
arousal 18, 28

bacteria 22–23, 24–25
baby fat 32
body hair 7, 8, 14–15, 16
body image 33–34
body mass index (BMI) 32, 35
body odor (BO) 8, 24
body parts (female)
  breasts 8, 10–11, 13
  clitoris 28
  fallopian tubes 12
  labia 8, 11
  nipples 8, 10, 28
  ovaries 8, 12, 28
  uterus 12–13
  vagina 8, 12, 13, 28
  vulva 8
body parts (male)
  Adam's apple 15
  breasts 16–17
  nipples 17
  penis 15, 16, 18, 28
  scrotum 16
  testes 14–15, 16
bra 10, 11
brain 6, 27, 38, 39

chemicals 6
cravings 13

dermabrasion 23
diet 8, 27, 32–33, 35, 36–37,
  38–39
drugs 16

eating disorders 34–35, 36–37,
  38
  anorexia nervosa 36–37
  binge eating 36
  bulimia nervosa 36–37
ejaculation 18
emotions 7, 13, 26–31, 36–37,
  39, 40–41
  mood swings 26–27, 38–39
  stress 22, 27, 38–39, 40–41
energy levels 7, 27, 32, 41
erection 16, 18, 28
exercise 9, 27, 32–33, 38–39

genes 22
genitals 25

glands 6
  adrenal glands 8, 14, 28
  pituitary gland 6
  sebaceous glands 20, 22–23
  sweat glands 15, 24, 25
    aprocrine glands 24
    eccrine glands 24
groin 24
growth spurt 6–7, 8, 14–15, 32

hair 15, 20, 22
health
  aching joints 8
  anemia 8
  asthma 32
  body dysmorphia 34
  bone and tooth decay 8
  cramps 13
  headaches 8, 13, 38
  heart disease 32
  high blood pressure 32
  muscle weakness 8
  nausea 8, 13
  obesity 8, 32–33, 36
  stomach aches 38
  testicular cancer 16
  tiredness 7, 8, 13, 27, 41
  type 2 diabetes 32
hips 8
hormones 6–7, 17, 26, 40
  androgen 14, 16, 20
  estrogen 8, 13, 16, 20
  progesterone 8
  sex hormones 7, 8, 12, 15, 20,
    28
  testosterone 14, 20, 28

immune system 37

laxatives 36
libido see sex drive

manic-depressive disorder 38
masturbation 18, 28
menopause 12
menstruation 6, 12–13, 20–21,
  22, 37
mental health 38–39
  anxiety disorder 38–39
  bipolar disorder 38–39
  depression 8, 38–39, 40–41
  obsessive compulsive disorder
  (OCD) 38
  schizophrenia 39

orgasm 18
ovulation 12

peer pressure 43
periods see menstruation
premenstrual syndrome (PMS) 13

relaxation 27, 39
reproduction 7, 18, 28

sebum 20, 22, 23
self-confidence 23, 42, 43
self-esteem 23, 34, 37, 40–41,
  42–43
self-harm 41
semen 18
sex drive 28
sexuality 30
  heterosexuality 30
  homosexuality 30–31
shaving
  boys 14–15
  girls 8–9
skin 20, 22–23, 24, 34
skin pores 20, 22
skin problems 8, 20–21, 22
  acne 20, 22–23, 34
  blackheads 20–21, 22
  cysts 22
  pimples 20-21, 22
  whiteheads 22
skin products 20–21, 23
sperm 12, 14, 18
sweat 8, 15, 24–25

tampons 13

vaginal discharge 8, 11
voice breaking 15
vomiting 8

washing 20–21, 23, 24–25, 38
waxing
  boys 15
  girls 8–9
weight
  gain 8, 32, 36–37
  loss 8, 35, 36-37
wet dream 18